CHELSEA FC

by Jeff Seidel

EUROPE'S BEST SOCCER CLUBS

SportsZone

An Imprint of Abdo Publishing
abdopublishing.com

abdopublishing.com

Published by Abdo Publishing, a division of ABDO, PO Box 398166, Minneapolis, Minnesota 55439. Copyright © 2018 by Abdo Consulting Group, Inc. International copyrights reserved in all countries. No part of this book may be reproduced in any form without written permission from the publisher. SportsZone™ is a trademark and logo of Abdo Publishing.

Printed in the United States of America, North Mankato, Minnesota
062017
092017

Cover Photos: Darren Walsh/ChelseaFC/AP Images, foreground; AP Images, background
Interior Photos: Alastair Grant/AP Images, 4; Alex James/JMP/Rex Features/AP Images, 7; BPI/Rex Features/AP Images, 9; Kirsty Wigglesworth/AP Images, 10; Peter Kemp/AP Images, 12; Press Association/URN:13447796/AP Images, 14; Picture Post/Hulton Archive/Getty Images, 17; AP Images, 18; Rebecca Naden/Press Association/URN:18454915/AP Images, 21; Frank Augstein/AP Images, 22; Julian Brown/Mirrorpix/Getty Images, 24; Darren Walsh/Chelsea FC/Getty Images, 27; David Klein/Cal Sport Media/AP Images, 28; Douglas Miller/Keystone/Hulton Archive/Getty Images, 30; Dave Caulkin/AP Images, 32; Christine Nesbitt/AP Images, 34; Sean Dempsey/Press Association/URN:19995632/AP Images, 37; Rex Features/AP Images, 38; McNulty/JMP/REX/Shutterstock/AP Images, 41; JasonPIX/REX/Shutterstock/AP Images, 42

Editor: Patrick Donnelly
Series Designer: Craig Hinton
Content Consultant: Paul Logothetis, European soccer reporter

Publisher's Cataloging-in-Publication Data

Names: Seidel, Jeff, author.
Title: Chelsea FC / by Jeff Seidel.
Description: Minneapolis, MN : Abdo Publishing, 2018. | Series: Europe's best soccer clubs | Includes bibliographical references and index.
Identifiers: LCCN 2016962216 | ISBN 9781532111334 (lib. bdg.) | ISBN 9781680789188 (ebook)
Subjects: LCSH: Soccer--Europe--History--Juvenile literature. | Soccer teams--Europe--History--Juvenile literature. | Soccer--Europe--Records--Juvenile literature. | Chelsea Football Club (Soccer team)--Juvenile literature.
Classification: DDC 796.334--dc23
LC record available at http://lccn.loc.gov/2016962216

TABLE OF
CONTENTS

Willian eludes Crystal Palace's Jordon Mutch during Chelsea's 2015 Premier League clincher.

CHAPTER 1

CHAMPIONS OF ENGLAND

Fans packed Stamford Bridge on May 3, 2015. The home stadium of the Chelsea Football Club (FC) was rocking. Chelsea midfielder Eden Hazard had scored on a header just before halftime. That was all the team needed to beat Crystal Palace 1–0. Chelsea had clinched its first Premier League championship in five years.

New Arrivals

Chelsea is one of the richest clubs in English soccer. The team won three Premier League titles between 2005 and 2010.

EUROPEAN SOCCER

The European soccer season is broken down into different levels of competition. It can be confusing to keep track. Here's a handy guide to help you follow the action.

League Play

The 20 best teams in England play in the Premier League. Teams play all league opponents twice each season for 38 total games. The three teams with the worst records are relegated—or sent down—to the second division, which sends three teams up to replace them the next season. The Premier League debuted in 1992–93. It replaced the Football League First Division (1888–1991) as England's top league.

European Play

The top four teams in the Premier League qualify for the Union of European Football Associations (UEFA) Champions League. This annual tournament involves the best teams from the top leagues throughout Europe. The Champions League started in 1992. It replaced the European Cup, a similar tournament that began in 1955.

The next three teams in the Premier League qualify for the UEFA Europa League. The Europa League is Europe's second-tier tournament. It runs in a similar manner to the Champions League but crowns its own winner. The Europa League debuted in 1971 as the UEFA Cup but was renamed in 2009.

Domestic Cups

Almost every English team is eligible to play for the Football Association Challenge Cup (FA Cup). The tournament typically includes several hundred teams, including the professional teams from the Premier League. Founded in 1871–72, the FA Cup is the oldest soccer tournament in the world. The League Cup is a similar tournament. It involves teams from only the top four divisions in England.

Chelsea's attack improved with Diego Costa's arrival from Spain.

But then the Blues hit a bit of a drought. The team still had some great players, such as defender John Terry, forward Didier Drogba, and midfielders Hazard and Willian. But the club hoped some new stars could inject new life into the team.

Before the 2014–15 season Chelsea signed midfielder Cesc Fàbregas and forward Diego Costa. Both players came from the Spanish league. Fàbregas had been with Barcelona, one of the best teams in Europe. Meanwhile, Costa had proved to be a goal-scoring dynamo for Atletico Madrid. Chelsea hoped the 25-year-old Costa could bring his goal-scoring instincts to west London.

Costa made an immediate impact that year. He scored in his first four Premier League games. The outburst included a two-goal game against Everton and a hat trick against Swansea City. Costa was named the Premier League player of the month in his first month with Chelsea. He went on to lead the team with 20 goals in league play that year.

Clear of the Field

Chelsea began to pull away from its closest rivals as the season progressed. It lost only three of 38 Premier League games. Chelsea's 26 victories and nine draws proved the Blues were the best team that season.

Eden Hazard, *10*, splits the Crystal Palace defense to score from a header.

A league title is every team's goal. The 2015 league title was especially timely for Chelsea. That year marked the 60th anniversary of the team's first title. It came in what was then called the First Division in 1954–55.

After their dominant start, the Blues needed to win one of their final three games to clinch the championship. They got it done on their first try. Hazard began the winning play

by missing a penalty kick. But Crystal Palace goalie Julian Speroni gave up a rebound. Hazard then slipped between the defense and headed the ball into the goal. He ran screaming in celebration at what turned out to be the championship-winning goal.

When the game ended, the celebrations began. The players came together for a big group hug. They waved to fans. Victory songs poured from loudspeakers. Streams of blue and white confetti fell from the sky. So did ticker tape. The scoreboard read "Champions 2014–15." The excitement continued the rest of the day and night.

The awards poured in after the season. José Mourinho earned Premier League Manager of the Season honors. Hazard won the Premier League Player of the Season Award. Costa, Hazard, midfielder Nemanja Matić, and defenders Terry, Gary Cahill, and Branislav Ivanović won another individual honor. They were named to the Professional Footballers' Association Team of the Year. That meant 6 of the 11 players on that team were from Chelsea.

Players and fans alike celebrate Chelsea's league-clinching victory.

11

Chelsea opened Stamford Bridge with a friendly against Liverpool in September 1905. Chelsea scored a 4–0 victory. From there, the team's popularity grew. More than 67,000 fans swarmed into Stamford Bridge to watch Chelsea play Manchester United on Good Friday in 1906. Chelsea was promoted to the First Division the following year. And the team continued to attract large crowds.

The Blues got their nickname early on. During the early years, the players wore Eton blue and white. They were the horse-racing colors of the club's then president, the Earl of Cadogan. Today, Chelsea's signature color is royal blue.

Chelsea has long featured some of the game's biggest stars. But it had a hard time winning championships. The Blues often finished in the middle of the pack. It took them a half-century to win a title.

Breaking Through

Chelsea finally snapped its long drought in its 50th season. The team became champions of English soccer in 1954–55. But that season started poorly. A four-game losing streak in October sent the Blues to the lower half of the standings. That soon changed, however.

Manager Ted Drake deserved a lot of the credit. Drake had been a striker with Arsenal. When he arrived in 1952, he changed the way Chelsea trained. Drake emphasized practicing with the ball. That tactic wasn't common in England at the time. Practices were more focused on fitness. Drake also scouted teams in the lower division and signed some of their lesser known but talented players. Drake changed a losing team into a winning one.

Chelsea locked up the 1955 league championship with a week to spare thanks to a 3–0 victory over Sheffield

Chelsea manager Ted Drake, *left*, talks with a reporter in 1952.

Wednesday. Roy Bentley, who was Chelsea's leading scorer for eight straight years, finished the season with a team-high 21 goals.

Chelsea fans storm the field after the Blues defeated Real Madrid to win the Cup Winners Cup in 1971.

More success followed after Drake left in 1961. Chelsea won the 1965 League Cup and reached the final of the 1967 FA Cup. In 1970 the Blues beat Leeds United 2–1 to win the FA Cup. Perhaps their greatest achievement came in 1971, when the Blues beat Real Madrid of Spain to win a tournament called the Cup Winners' Cup.

However, hard times then fell upon the club. The Blues bounced between the First and Second Divisions in the 1970s and 1980s. With the club in debt and facing extinction, the Mears family had to sell in 1982.

New Life

In 1988–89 Chelsea won the Second Division championship. That sent the Blues back to the First Division. From then on, the team never looked back. Chelsea won the 1997 FA Cup. Once again the Blues were a threat to win in every competition.

Then, in 2003, everything changed. Chelsea, facing financial struggles, beat Liverpool on the final game of the 2002–03 season. The win meant the Blues had qualified for the next season's Champions League. That win helped stabilize the team's finances.

Soon after, Russian billionaire Roman Abramovich bought the club. He had huge expectations. He believed

FAST FACT
Antonio Conte took over as Chelsea's manager in 2016 and became just the fourth manager to win the Premier League title in his first attempt. A successful player and manager at Juventus, Conte also led Italy's national team from 2014 to 2016.

Chelsea could one day win the Champions League and be called the best team in Europe. To get there, Abramovich began injecting money into the team.

Chelsea looked to the best leagues in the world to find players. International stars such as goalie Petr Čech, midfielder Claude Makelele, and forward Didier Drogba came aboard. They joined English stars John Terry, Joe Cole, and Frank Lampard. To lead the group, Chelsea hired bold young manager José Mourinho in 2004–05. He had led Porto, a team from his native Portugal, to the Champions League title the previous season.

The changes within the club were drastic. It was great news for Chelsea fans. But others around England were less thrilled. Many people were put off when Mourinho called himself the "special one" before his first season. But he lived up to his own hype. Chelsea won the league for the first time in 50 years in 2004–05. And then it won the league again the next year.

Players came and left over the next several years. Mourinho even left, came back, and then left once more. But since 2005 Chelsea has been consistently one of Europe's best teams. The

The arrival of forward Didier Drogba, left, and manager José Mourinho helped Chelsea establish itself as a power in English soccer.

Blues won the Premier League again in 2009–10, 2014–15, and 2016–17. They won the FA Cup in 2007, 2009, 2010, and 2012.

What they really wanted, though, was to win the Champions League. Under Abramovich, Chelsea became a regular in the tournament. In 2008 the Blues reached the final against English rival Manchester United. The game ended in heartbreak for Chelsea. After playing to a 1–1 draw in Moscow, Russia, the teams settled it in a shootout. Longtime Chelsea star Terry had a chance to win the game, but he slipped on his kick. The shot bounced off the post. Two rounds later, Manchester United was the champion of Europe.

The Blues would have their day, though. Four years later, in 2012, they made it back to the Champions League final. This time, playing against German club Bayern Munich in Munich, Chelsea prevailed. The game was once again a 1–1 draw through 120 minutes. But Drogba converted the last kick in the shootout to bring the trophy to a London team for the first time. It might have taken longer than he expected, but Abramovich's bold vision had finally been achieved.

Drogba celebrates after scoring late in regulation to tie Bayern Munich in the 2012 Champions League final.

CHAPTER 3

THE BEAUTIFUL PEOPLE

Soccer is viewed as a sport for everyone. You don't need a lot of money to play soccer. In England the sport has been uniquely popular with the working class since the 1800s.

Naturally, many Chelsea fans came from the working class. But the team also attracts fans from England's wealthy and fashionable elite. The Chelsea neighborhood is the draw. In the 1960s the neighborhood was the center of the youth revolution. It became fashionable for musicians, models, and movie stars to show up at Stamford Bridge to root for the Blues. Movie stars

Michael Caine and Raquel Welch often graced the stands. The club symbolized glamour and class.

Those traditions continue today. The Chelsea neighborhood is home to stylish shops, trendy cafes, and modern music. Celebrity fans include comedian Will Farrell and chef Gordon Ramsay.

Not surprisingly, jealousy often comes with the spotlight. Chelsea became known as the "most hated team in England." Fans of other clubs resented Chelsea supporters' wealth and standing in society. They also resented the club's high payroll. Chelsea spends large sums of money to sign the best players. Clubs with far less money cry foul. It makes Chelsea an easy target for rivals.

FAST FACT

Chelsea became the first English soccer club to start a full lineup of players not from England. It happened in a game against Southampton on December 26, 1999.

Rivals

Chelsea has a history of fierce battles with top foes throughout England. Their fellow west London clubs—Fulham, Brentford,

Celebrity chef Gordon Ramsay and his son Jack greet Chelsea captain John Terry before a 2009 game.

and Queens Park Rangers—are not among them. That's because those teams have often been in different divisions.

The Blues' rivals include Tottenham Hotspur and West Ham United. For many years, Chelsea and West Ham's stadiums were both off the District Line train. The "District Line Derby" got particularly tense in the early 2000s. This happened after Chelsea bought some of West Ham's top young players.

Chelsea's rivalry with Arsenal dates back to the 1930s. It heated up in the early 2000s. Arsenal won the Premier League

without a loss in 2003–04, holding off second-place Chelsea. Then José Mourinho arrived at Chelsea. The Blues won the next two league titles. The two clubs have been among the best in Europe ever since.

Meanwhile, Chelsea has had rivalries with teams outside of London. In the 1960s and 1970s, Chelsea and Leeds United played many big matches. The biggest came in the 1970 FA Cup. Chelsea won a rough two-game final. More recently, Chelsea and Manchester United have battled for the Premier League title. In 2008, the English teams even met in the Champions League final. Manchester United won in a shootout. Another twist was added to the rivalry when Manchester United hired Mourinho as its new manager in 2016.

It's always a tense, physical battle when Chelsea and Manchester United square off.

CHAPTER 4

STARS OF THE PAST

Chelsea has fielded numbers of superstar players. Even in down years, the Blues have featured stars who kept the stands rocking at Stamford Bridge.

Early Days

Forward Jack Cock is considered Chelsea's first major star. He played four years with Chelsea. He joined the team after serving with distinction in World War I (1914–1918). Cock scored 22 goals in his first season. He became a fan favorite. Cock made a name

Peter Osgood, *left*, blasts a shot past the Everton keeper in 1973.

for himself off the field too. He sang and acted in movies such as *The Winning Goal* and *The Great Game*.

Only two players have served as a captain when Chelsea won a League Championship. Forward Roy Bentley was the first. He joined the team from Newcastle in 1948. Bentley was the Blues' leading scorer when they won their first league championship as a team. He scored 150 goals in his career. Bentley always seemed to give Chelsea a spark on the field.

Forward Peter Osgood was another Chelsea legend. "The King of Stamford Bridge" scored two goals in his debut as a 17-year-old. He went on to lead the team to its 1970 FA Cup triumph. Osgood played at Stamford Bridge from 1964 to 1974. He returned from 1978 to 1979.

International Flavor

After some down years, Chelsea began to thrive again in the 1990s. That success came in large part to players from other countries, even as most Premier League players were still British.

In 1995 Chelsea signed Dutch midfielder Ruud Gullit, a former World Player of the Year. One year later, Gullit became the team's player-manager. He brought in more international stars, including French defender Frank Leboeuf, as well as midfielder Roberto Di Matteo and forward Gianluca Vialli, both from Italy.

The biggest name was Italian midfielder Gianfranco Zola. The 5-foot-6-inch forward immediately dazzled the fans at Stamford Bridge. Between 1996 and 2003, Zola scored 80

goals while leading the Blues to six trophies. He is also credited with helping young players such as John Terry and Frank Lampard develop into stars.

Zola left Chelsea after the 2002–03 season to finish his career at his home club in Italy. However, he left Chelsea on strong footing. The club had been losing money. But it finished fourth in the league that season. That meant Chelsea qualified for the Champions League for only the second time in team history. Fans at Stamford Bridge still sing songs about Zola.

A Special Era

Zola left Chelsea in a good place. Russian billionaire Roman Abramovich stepped in to take the team even higher. When he bought the club in 2003, Chelsea already had star

Gianfranco Zola was small in stature but a big hit with Chelsea fans.

players such as Terry and Lampard. Abramovich signed even more to the roster.

FAST FACT

During Chelsea's Premier League championship season of 2004–05, Petr Čech did not give up a goal for a record 1,025 minutes.

Petr Čech joined the Blues in 2004. He was one of the top goalies in all of Europe. Čech helped lead the team to Premier League titles in his first two seasons. Chelsea fans would soon get used to that sight. With the Czech goalie manning the back line, Chelsea won two more Premier League titles, four FA Cups, and the 2012 Champions League Final. Before leaving Chelsea in 2015, Čech played in 494 games for the Blues.

Didier Drogba also joined Chelsea in 2004. The Ivory Coast native quickly became a goal-scoring machine for the Blues. Using his big body to get into position, Drogba became one of the league's most dominant forwards. He scored 100 goals in Premier League play over eight seasons. No other African player had done that. After two seasons away, Drogba returned to Chelsea for one more season in 2014–15. He was

Frank Lampard was a dominant midfielder and a huge part of Chelsea's resurgence under new owner Roman Abramovich.

particularly effective in European play, scoring 36 career goals in those competitions.

Drogba had plenty of help in the scoring department, especially from midfielders Frank Lampard and Michael Essien. Lampard joined Chelsea in 2001 and was a fixture at midfield for the next 13 seasons. With a booming shot, Lampard set a club record with 211 goals in all competitions. Essien joined the team in 2005. He proved to be a force in Chelsea's midfield before leaving in 2014.

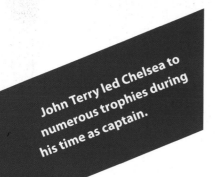

CHAPTER 5

MODERN STARS

Players such as Petr Čech, Didier Drogba, and Frank Lampard helped turn Chelsea into a European power. A new generation helped Chelsea maintain that status. Longtime team captain John Terry played a role in both eras.

Terry is the most successful captain in team history. He joined the team in 1998 and became captain just before his 21st birthday in 2001. The center back quickly worked his way into Chelsea's starting lineup. With his tough and disciplined play, he won numerous awards. He was selected to the World Team of the Year every year from 2005 to 2009. Terry played with the Blues through the 2016–17 season. His name is synonymous with Chelsea.

The New Guard

Chelsea reached a high point with its Champions League victory in 2012. That squad was made up of a lot of veteran players. Spanish midfielder Juan Mata played a major role in the win. But he would need reinforcements if Chelsea was to continue to thrive. So during that offseason, Chelsea signed midfielder Eden Hazard. At age 21, the Belgian midfielder was one of the brightest young stars in the game. He proved to be one of the team's best players.

Hazard led Chelsea in goals in just his second season in England. He was named the team's Player of the Year. His biggest goal came in 2014–15 to lock up the Premier League title. Hazard earned Footballer of the Year honors from England's Football Writers' Association that season. And he won the Barclays Premier League Player of the Year Award.

FAST FACT
Terry is just the third player in Chelsea history to play in 700 games for the club.

Eden Hazard celebrates a goal against Manchester City in 2016.

Hazard has gotten help from some talented teammates. After arriving from Barcelona in 2014, Cesc Fàbregas made big contributions immediately. The midfielder registered two assists in his first match. He proved himself to be an incredibly gifted and versatile player. Fàbregas has often shifted forward to play striker when needed. He scored five goals in 2014–15 when the team won the Premier League championship.

Diego Costa joined Chelsea from Atletico Madrid in Spain on July 15, 2014. The move proved to be a good one as Chelsea won the Premier League title during his first season. He scored nine goals in his first seven league matches and ended the year as the league's top scorer with 20 goals. The Blues stumbled the next season, falling far off the pace and losing their manager. But Costa again ended up as the team's top scorer, posting 16 goals overall.

After a down season in 2015-16, the Blues' stars were back in top form in 2016-17. Fellow players voted four Chelsea stars to the league's best 11. They were defenders David Luiz and Gary Cahill, and midfielders N'Golo Kante and Hazard. Kante was named player of the year. So it was no surprise that the Blues ended the season with their fifth Premier League title.

Spaniards Cesc Fàbregas, top, and Diego Costa gave the Chelsea lineup a jolt when they joined the Blues in 2014.

CHELSEA FC
TEAM FILE

NAME: Chelsea FC

YEAR FORMED: 1905

WHERE THEY PLAY: Stamford Bridge, London, England

FOOTBALL LEAGUE/PREMIER LEAGUE TITLES: 6
(most recent in 2016–17)

FA CUPS: 7 (most recent in 2012)

LEAGUE CUPS: 5
(most recent in 2015)

UEFA CHAMPIONS LEAGUE TITLES: 1 (2012)

UEFA EUROPA LEAGUE TITLES: 1 (2013)

AUTHOR'S DREAM TEAM

GOALKEEPER: Petr Čech

DEFENSE: Peter Sillett, John Terry, Stan Willemse

MIDFIELD: Marcel Desailly, Frank Lampard, Gianfranco Zola, Charlie Cooke

FORWARDS: Didier Drogba, Jimmy Greaves, Peter Osgood

KEY RECORDS

- Most career goals: Frank Lampard, 211

- Largest margin of victory (top flight level): 8–0 vs. Wigan, 2010; 8–0 vs. Aston Villa, 2012

- Longest league winning streak: 11 games, April 25–September 26, 2009

TIMELINE

1905

Chelsea FC is founded in a London pub.

1952

Chelsea brings in Ted Drake as the team's manager.

1955

Chelsea breaks through after a 50-year dry spell and wins its first league championship.

1970

Chelsea defeats Leeds United 2–1 to win its first FA Cup.

1997

Led by Gianfranco Zola and other stars, Chelsea wins the FA Cup.

2003

Russian billionaire Roman Abramovich buys Chelsea and the club begins spending a lot more money on players.

2005

Chelsea wins the Premier League title. It's the team's first league title in 50 years.

2008

After playing to a 1–1 draw, Chelsea loses to Manchester United on penalty kicks in the Champions League final.

2012

Chelsea beats Bayern Munich of Germany in a shootout to win its first Champions League title.

2013

Manager José Mourinho, who led Chelsea to its first two Premier League titles, returns to Chelsea.

2017

Chelsea finishes seven points clear of Tottenham Hotspur to clinch its fifth Premier League title since 2005.

GLOSSARY

club

The team a player competes with outside of his or her national team.

debut

First appearance.

drought

A long period without success.

forward

Also called a striker, the player who plays nearest the opponent's goal.

friendly

A match that is not part of league play or a tournament; an exhibition match.

generation

A group of people who are similar in age and other identifying characteristics.

hat trick

Three goals in a game scored by the same player.

midfielder

A player who stays mostly in the middle third of the field and links the defenders with the forwards.

penalty kick

A free kick at the goal, defended only by the keeper, awarded after a foul in the penalty area; also used to break ties in a shootout.

promoted

Moved up from a lower level of competition to a stronger league.

rivals

Opponents with whom a player or team has a fierce and ongoing competition.

scouted

Looked for talented players on other teams.

stabilize

To control and maintain consistency.

FOR MORE INFORMATION

BOOKS

Kortemeier, Todd. *Make Me the Best Soccer Player*. Minneapolis, MN: Abdo Publishing, 2017.

Marthaler, Jon. *Soccer Trivia*. Minneapolis, MN: Abdo Publishing, 2016.

McDougall, Chrös. *The Best Soccer Players of All Time*. Minneapolis, MN: Abdo Publishing, 2015.

WEBSITES

To learn more about Chelsea, visit abdobooklinks.com. These links are routinely monitored and updated to provide the most current information available.

PLACE TO VISIT

STAMFORD BRIDGE

Fulham Road, London SW6, 1HS, United Kingdom
Phone: +44 20 7386 9373
chelseafc.com/the-club/stadium-tours-and-museum.html

Go behind the scenes at the stadium where Chelsea has played since 1906. Tour all parts of the stadium, relive club history at the Stamford Bridge museum, and load up on the latest Chelsea gear at the team store.

INDEX

ABOUT THE AUTHOR

Jeff Seidel has been a journalist for the past 30 years in the Baltimore/Washington, DC, area. He's written books on baseball, football, college football, and soccer. He lives in Baltimore with his family and two cats, Buddy and Albie.